LIFE CHANGING BOOK

MEANING OF LIFE

Do You Know The One Thing You've Been Missing?

Victor Greene

Table of Contents

Chapter 1: Living Life Without Regrets 6

Chapter 2: Live Life To The Fullest 8

Chapter 3: Making Sky The Limit 10

Chapter 4: The Danger Of Dwelling On Things 12

Chapter 5: How To Succeed In Life Before Quitting 15

Chapter 6: The Keys To Happiness 18

Chapter 7: 20 Positive Affirmations For Men 21

Chapter 8: How Your Beliefs And Moods Contribute To What's Going On In Your Life 25

Chapter 9: Other People's Problems Are Not Always Your Problems 28

Chapter 10: How To Train Yourself to Be Optimistic and Positive ... 31

Chapter 11: Why You Should Measure Everything 34

Chapter 12: Why Getting Started Is More Important Than Succeeding 37

Chapter 13: Why Nobody Cares When You Fail 40

Chapter 14: 10 Life Skills That Men Need to Have 43

Chapter 15: It's All About Networking 47

Chapter 16: How To Develop An Incredible Work Ethic 49

Chapter 17: How To Stop Judging Your Own Work 53

Chapter 18: 3 Steps To Choose Mind Over Mood 57

Chapter 19: 8 Ways To Turn Stress Into Strength 61

Chapter 20: How To Spend Money Wisely 65

Chapter 21: 6 Ways To Get More Attention 68

Chapter 22: 9 Tips To Reduce Stress 72

Chapter 23: When It Is Time To Slow Down 76

Chapter 24: 10 Work From Home Hacks 79

Chapter 25: 6 Ways To Master Your Emotions 82

Chapter 26: 3 Ways To Master Your Next Move 87

Chapter 27: 3 Ways To Calm The Emotional Storm Within You 90

Chapter 28: 6 Ways To Achieve Peak Performance 94

Chapter 29: 10 Stress Management Tips 98

Chapter 30: How To Deal With Impatience 102

Chapter 31: How To Tell It's Time To Move On From Your Job Or Switch Careers   105

Chapter 32: How To Play The Long Game In Life 108

Chapter 33: 16 Steps To Stop Feeling Like Shit 110

Chapter 34: 20 Affirmations For Women 114

Chapter 1:
Living Life Without Regrets

As Mick Jagger once said, "the past is a great place and I don't want to erase it or to regret it, but I don't want to be its prisoner either." Regret is like an uninvited ghost, and it likes to make an appearance when we are at our lowest. It dwells in the back of our heads from time to time and reminds us of the things that we wish we had done differently in our lives. But, just like a million other things and emotions, regrets only stay with us if we feed on it and let it in. It can be A heavy burden for us to carry, so in order to get rid of this lingering ghost, it's essential that we first understand what we are actually regretting and why.

If your life were about to end tomorrow - if that drunk doesn't stop at the red light, or the meteor is headed right for your house, would you go into your memory and start seeing your regrets? Or would you just accept it all and wish that you had lived your life more freely? Trust me when I say this, it's really okay to screw up. We're not people who can't make any mistakes and be flawless. Take A hurdler in the olympics as an example; he knocks over about half of the hurdles in that 110 metres, and they don't even break stride. Because at the end, it's not about not knocking over any hurdles or running the perfect race, it all comes down to getting across the line. So don't ever fear or regret failing - you give it A shot, and that's all that matters in the end.

We all know how Michael Jordan struggled with his career. In his own words, "I've missed more than 9000 shots in my career. I've lost almost 3000 games. 26 times, I've been trusted to take the game winning shot and missed. I've failed over and over and over again in my life. And that's why I succeed." Had he given up in his first try, the world would have never known A legend like him. He must've had A thousand second thoughts every time he failed, he must've regretted opting basketball every time he lost A game, but he kept going and never gave up. We should have A similar outlook on our lives. No matter what we did in our past, or whatever our decisions were that led to what we are now, it all must have A connection or A meaning. We just have to stop, think, and analyze.

Now, the first step to explore the space of your mind and begin addressing the things that you regret, is to have A conversation with yourself. But keep in mind, this isn't A blame game and it definitely isn't meant for you to slip down into A rabbit hole of self-sabotage. Holding onto regret is one form of self-sabotaging, but you should move forward by identifying things that are working against you and having healthier conversations with yourself to get to the root of things. Regret is A powerful emotion, it can consume your thoughts, energy, and time. Feeling miserable is totally fine as long as you keep A check on yourself and don't let it drain you completely. No matter what your situation is, you can work on this "ghost of regret" to leave by starting doing positive things for yourself. Feed your life with passion and love, and regrets will say good-bye to you soon.

Chapter 2:
Live Life To The Fullest

Have you ever felt like others don't understand your pain when they seem to be living a happy life? You're not alone in feeling this way, but the truth is that happiness takes work, and learning how to live life to the fullest takes dedication and practice.

People who smile in public have been through every bit as much as people who cry, frown, and scream. They just simply found the courage and strength to smile through it and enjoy life in the best way possible.

Life is short, and we only live once. Learning to live life to the fullest is an important step in making the most of every day.

Whether it's taking care of your children, working hard on your career, writing a new blog post each day, or baking up fabulous creations, you get to decide how you enjoy spending your time. Your parents, friends, community, and society in general all have their opinions, but at the end of the day, you're the only person who will be around for every moment of your life.

Do what makes you happy, and everything else will fall into place. This may not mean finding your perfect job if you're limited by education, location, or job openings. However, you can still do what you love by engaging in hobbies, volunteer work, or mentoring.

Sometimes there's danger involved in life, but every reward carries risk with it. If you never take risks, you'll never get anywhere in life, and you certainly won't learn how to live life to the fullest.

Staying in your comfort zone is the fastest way to become discontent Without stepping outside what you're already comfortable with, you will cease to learn and stagnate in both your personal and professional life. While it may feel uncomfortable, taking a risk can be as simple as saying yes next time your friends want to go out instead of staying at home alone. It can mean going out on a blind date, buying plane tickets to a new city, or dragging out those paints that have been stuffed away for years.

When people look back on their lives, they regret the chances they didn't take more than the ones they did, so find something new to try today and set goals beyond what you currently believe possible.

You'll hear people say, "I had that idea," every time you see someone create something great. Everyone had the idea for Facebook first. The reason Mark Zuckerberg got rich off of it is because he went out and did it while everyone else was talking about it. Learning to live life to the fullest is a big step in discovering a path that will lead you to your greatest sense of happiness and accomplishment. We all need moments to rest and relish in a sense of contentment, but staying in one place too long will leave you feeling a lack in life. Discover what makes your life feel meaningful and go after it.

Chapter 3:
Making Sky The Limit

Your attitude determines everything, whether it's in your personal life or your professional one. You ask any millionaire or billionaire how they got on top of their game and how they got to where they are, and they will undoubtedly tell you that they mastered their mind before mastering their game of success. So, the question arises, what exactly do we need to do to get to the next level? Some people strive for bigger things and achieve their goals against all odds, and they are not at all constrained by conventional thinking. Irrespective of their area of interest and chosen fields, they have certain experiences and characteristics in common. We now look at some of the things that we need to maintain to have a sky's-the-limit mindset.

Mastering your mind for the sky's-the-limit mindset comes up with the most crucial key, accepting rejection. We all have faced and experienced rejection at some point in our lives. But if we let it consume us and allow it to fester, it can lie dormant and negatively affect our lives. There are a million examples in front of us who faced rejections but are now extremely successful. Take J.K. Rowling; she was a single mother living on welfare and struggling to support her child. She faced repeated rejections but never gave up. Her first Harry Potter book got sold for about €4000. Now she's even richer than the Queen of England.

We all want to be successful, but are we ready to put in the blood, sweat, and tears it takes to get there? Thinking big and doing big takes willpower and a lot of work, the amount of work that isn't a piece of cake for everyone. Malcolm Gladwell tells us that if you want to be an expert or champion in something, you must be willing to devote 10,000 hours to it (90 minutes a day for 20 years). And if you're doing so, you need to feel passionate about it too. Van Gogh sold only one piece during his lifetime, but his passion drove him to paint almost 900 works.

Understand that we are flawed creatures, and we are bound to make mistakes. Bill Gates may be the world's richest man, but even he says that his failures served him as a great learning tool. Thomas Edison took between 1,000 to 10,000 tries before creating the world-changing invention. See your failures as a part of your journey. Without them, you won't be able to succeed much. And if they can fail, what makes you think you can't?

Be confident in your abilities and trust yourself. Surround yourself with good people who will help you accomplish things. People who would clap at your success and help you during your failures. Welcome every opportunity with open arms. Find the good in every situation, no matter how bad it looks on the outside. Every experience has its value, identify and cherish those experiences that serve you with opportunities to learn. The only thing stopping you from being successful is yourself.

Chapter 4:
The Danger Of Dwelling On Things

Do you ever go through a phase where you constantly replay old events in your head or worry and fret about what you could have done differently in a particular situation? Or do you obsessively dwell on past events and keep on repeating a loop of overthinking about your problems? Well, you might think that you're being productive by trying to solve your issues, but in reality, it does more harm than good to you.

There is a specific word for the above situation, and it is "Rumination." Ruminating is the process of dwelling on past events that can't be changed. People who have an anxiety-prone personality are more likely to experience this than others. Some examples include replaying conversations, repeating the past negative experiences in your mind, dwelling on injuries or injustices, and always asking seemingly unanswerable questions of "why me?" In all instances of rumination, the point is that the person gets stuck on a single subject, experience, or emotion.

Yale University conducted research that showed women are more likely to ruminate than men, leading to women having a higher risk of depression. Additionally, the study also focused on the fact that rumination prevents people from acknowledging and dealing with their emotions; they try to understand the situation instead of focusing on the feelings that the situation has caused. The impact of rumination is dangerous and is often underestimated. It is also given the name of "the silent mental health problem." It can play a significant role in anything from obsessive-compulsive disorder (OCD) to eating disorders. According to the World Health Organization (WHO), mental health affects one person in every four during their lifetime and is the leading cause of disability globally. In 2010 alone, they were estimated to have cost $2.5 trillion globally by the World Economic Forum.

Dwelling your past and never escaping the loop will affect you negatively that will eventually eat you alive. Some things might help you to overcome this problem. The first is to self-evaluate and dedicate time to whatever it is that's bothering you. Write all your thoughts down on a piece of paper or the notes app on your phone, and set aside some time to think about it. Imagine the worst-case scenario that could happen from your dwelling, and then find a way that how you will deal with it. It will eventually leave you calmer and less anxious because a solution would already be in your hands.

Identify your anxiety triggers and the patterns that eventually lead you to rumination. Once you have identified it, focus on what you would do the next time to avoid making those mistakes again. Talking to a friend would be a good solution too. Write about the things that make you happy and the things you are grateful for. Revisit the list every day and focus on the positives.

It may be easier said than done, but accept that everyone makes mistakes, and it's in the past. You have learned from the situations, and now you have to let go and move on. It may not be easy at first but practice it every day. The more you practice, the easier this process will become, and you will eventually find your peace.

Chapter 5:
How To Succeed In Life Before Quitting

Getting rid of a job is always risky, especially if you want to succeed in life. Sometimes we have to choose our satisfactory activity even if we are settled for something else. But you have to keep in mind that these risks might be worth pursuing your dreams. You should have confidence in yourself if you are letting go of your stable job. You are starting by taking small baby steps and keeping a clear idea in your mind of what you want or if quitting your job is the right decision.

When wanting to quit a full-time job, you need to make sure of some things first. One of them is financial stability. It's not something you can leave on its own. Taking care of your finances should be your first step as it will help you in further needs. Try not to ask for help much. Make yourself capable of purchasing your needs and wants.

To be a successful person, the most important thing is not to be afraid of failure. You have to plant courage and confidence in your mind. Quitting will be easier when you know what you are doing. It keeps you aware of your needs and makes your decision stronger. You cannot second guess yourself if you make the right choice. Be willing to fail ever once in a while.

Positivity in life is an easier way to be successful. Take everything lightly and make sure that negativity gets ignored. You cannot get discouraged if people don't support your ideas and goals. Suppose you feel like you should quit. Go for it. The world will not see the journey, but the results will be visualized clearly for them. So, keep positivity in your mind and heart.

Becoming a successful person comes with a lot to take in, and it might not be as easy as it will have seemed. So, the smartest move that anyone can make is to take their time while making any decision in this regard. So should weigh all of your options while keeping your mental and physical health in check. Choose the best one for yourself always.

You should be ready for anything that comes your way. Don't be scared of rejection. Don't be scared of others' opinions. Even ask for advice from someone if you need help in deciding. Ask your superiors for guidance in this regard. Let people motivate you for a greater cause. And better, motivate yourself. The secret to success is to enjoy your work. If you work thinking that you will earn only or become powerful only, you are wrong. You will be stuck in one place for a long time. You need to make sure to have fun along the way. That way, everything you do will be worth it.

Becoming successful before quitting can be quite challenging, but that is one way to become yourself. You are getting a focused view of what you want in life and how you'll work things out. Just make sure to have all the right ingredients you'll need to quit one part of your life to start a new one. And hopefully a better part of your life for yourself.

Chapter 6:
The Keys To Happiness

If I ask you "what is happiness?", then what would your answer be? It's probably difficult to come up with a simple answer. Yet, here you are, looking for a key to happiness and how to lead a fulfilling life.
The truth is that a universal key to happiness is a myth.

That doesn't mean that you should stop looking for yours right now, it only means that you need to be careful when reading articles about "a key to happiness". The universal key to happiness is non-existent because happiness is one of the most difficult things in life to define.
Now, let's go back to that difficult question: "what is happiness?"
Have you thought about it already? Let me give you an example of how hard it is to define happiness.

Right now, I'm drinking a cup of coffee while writing the outline of this article about how to define happiness. Am I happy right now? Yes, I'm feeling pretty happy:

- I've got nothing to worry about.
- All my basic needs are met.
- The weather is nice.
- I'm going outside in a couple of minutes to go for a walk.
-

These things are all making me feel pretty happy right now.

By that logic, let's define my happiness as follows:

"Happiness is when I'm in a worry-free state, the weather is nice, everybody I know is alright and I can enjoy a hot cup of coffee."

Voila. There it is. My definition of happiness.

The keys to my happiness are obvious now, and I know enough in order to lead the happiest life I can. I just need to focus on the things I listed above.

Wait a second… If it were this simple, then why have I ever been unhappy?

You might have guessed it already, but I made a very simple error. I assumed that what makes me happy today will make me happy for the rest of my life. And that's just wrong.

Happiness is something that not only changes from person to person, but it's also constantly evolving from day to day.

Your definition of happiness changes over time. This is why happiness is such a difficult concept, and why there's not a single "key to happiness".

Whoever tells you otherwise is likely not aware that people change, and that people don't always share the same values, goals, and purposes.

For a minute, I want you to do consider your own happiness. I want you to think back of last week, and consider what things you did that had a positive effect on your happiness.

What things had a significant influence on your mood? What comes to your mind?

Was it spending time with your friends? Was it a great movie you watched? Did you attend an exciting sports event? Or did you enjoy sipping hot coffee on a sunny Wednesday morning? It could obviously be just about anything!

The most important thing to remember when trying to define your keys to a happy and fulfilling life is simple:
There is no universal key that leads to your happiness. That's because your happiness is unique in each and every single way

Chapter 7:
20 Positive Affirmations For Men

A positive affirmation is a statement about yourself that is phrased in the positive, present tense. It reflects an area of your life, emotions, or belief system that you want to improve or change. The potential benefits of affirmations are vast. Positive affirmations empower you to become the best version of yourself. They inspire you to act in ways that help you fulfill your potential. You can use positive affirmations to reprogram negative thoughts into positive beliefs. The ability to reprogram your beliefs about yourself has the potential to transform your life completely.

For an affirmation to be effective, it needs to meet four criteria.

Each positive affirmation you use should be:

1. **Worded in the present tense**
2. **Positive**
3. **Specific**
4. **Personal**

You can create your own positive affirmations using this four-step framework. The benefits of affirmations are dramatically increased when you have created it yourself from an existing negative belief. Let's say you had a belief that you are unsuccessful in your job. Where focus goes, energy flows. If you keep feeding this belief, it will manifest as truth.

When you understand this, you can see how our thoughts really do shape our reality. Instead, you can use this belief as an opportunity to grow. Take that statement and switch it to its positive opposite. Rather than thinking: 'I am terrible at my job, I'll never get a promotion, my boss hates me,' you now think 'I am great at my job, I love what I do, and I always put 100% effort into every task

Whether you choose to formulate your own positive affirmations or use the ones I have created for you below, you must cultivate a daily practice. The best times to practice are first thing in the morning and last thing at night (or whenever you feel that you need to repeat them to start feeling better). During these times, your mind is more open and will absorb the statements on a deeper level.

It is best if you say them out loud while looking in the mirror. Speaking them to yourself affirms that you trust in yourself, and you believe the statements to be true. If speaking them out loud is not possible, you can say them in your mind. Writing them out a few times a week is also beneficial. Try getting a journal specifically for this purpose. Another technique that you might find useful is to pin the written affirmations to the mirror or refrigerator, where you will see them often.

When you are just beginning with this practice, it may be easy to forget, so set an alert on your phone or in your calendar to remind you. Here are 20 examples of positive affirmations relating to different areas of life.

Choose the ones that resonate most with you. Once you feel that you have integrated those particular statements, you can select or create new ones for other areas you want to improve.

Confidence and Self-Esteem

1: "I feel confident in every situation."

2: "I like who I am."

3: "I am a good person."

4: "I am great at helping people."

5: "I feel valued by my friends and family."

Inner Strength and Resilience

1: "I meet each new challenge with enthusiasm."

2: "I am strong and stable."

3: "I think I can, so I can."

4: "No matter what happens, I can handle it."

5: "I am powerful."

Positivity and Joy

1: **"I radiate joy to everyone I meet."**

2: **"I see the best in people."**

3: **"In the present moment there are no issues, only peace."**

4: **"Happiness is a choice; today, I choose to be happy."**

5: **"I have the power to turn negative thoughts into positive beliefs."**

Career and Success

1: **"I deserve success."**

2: "I can succeed at whatever I choose."

3: "I am good at my job, and I love what I do."

4: "I have great ideas."

5: "I am innovative and tenacious."

I hope that my guide to positive affirmations for men has provided you with a solid foundation for designing your perfect practice. Remember, to reap the benefits of affirmations, you should say them out loud every day and write them out a few times a week. Use any of my examples of positive affirmations, or for extra power, try creating your own using my framework. If you commit to a daily practice, you will soon notice the benefits in your career, relationships, emotional resilience, sense of self-worth, and confidence.

Chapter 8:
How Your Beliefs And Moods Contribute To What's Going On In Your Life

Because our ability to successfully interact with other people is so important to our survival, these skills have become part of human nature. We determine whether to help in large part on the basis of how other people make us feel, and how we think we will feel if we help or do not help them.

Positive Moods Increase, Helping

I do not need to tell you that people help more when they are in good mood. We ask our parents to use their car, and we ask our boss for a raise, when we think they are in a positive mood rather than a negative one. Positive moods have been shown to increase many types of helping behavior, including contributing to charity, donating blood, and helping coworkers (isen, 1999). It is also relatively easy to put people in a good mood. You might not be surprised to hear that people are more likely to help after they've done well on a test or just received a big bonus in their paycheck. But research has found that even more trivial things, such as finding a coin in a phone booth, listening to a comedy recording, having someone smile at you, or even smelling the pleasant scent of perfume is enough to put people in a good mood and to cause them to be helpful (baron & thomley, 1994; gueguen & de gail, 2003; isen & levin, 1972).

In another study, van baaren, holland, kawakami, and van knippenberg (2004) had students interact with an experimenter who either mimicked them by subtly copying their behaviors outside of their awareness or did not mimic them. The researchers found that people who had been mimicked were more likely to help, by picking up pens that had fallen on the floor and by donating to a charity. It is quite possible that this effect is due to the influence of positive moods on helping—we like people we see as similar to us and that puts us in a good mood, making us more likely to help. In sum, the influence of mood on helping is substantial (carlson, charlin, & miller, 1988), so if you're looking for help, ask on a nice day, subtly mimic the person's behaviors, or prepare some good jokes.

But why does being in a good mood make us helpful? There are probably several reasons. For one, a positive mood indicates that the environment is not dangerous and therefore that we can safely help others. Second, we like other people more when we are in good moods, and that may lead us to help them. Finally, and perhaps most important, is the possibility the helping makes us feel good about ourselves, thereby maintaining our positive mood. In fact, people who are in good moods are particularly likely to help when the help that they are going to give seems likely to maintain their positive mood. But if they think that the helping is going spoil their good mood, even people in good moods are likely to refuse to help (erber & markunas, 2006).

In the end, we cannot completely rule out the possibility that people help in large part for selfish reasons. But does it really matter? If we give money to the needy because we will feel bad about ourselves if we do not, or if we give money to the needy because we want them to feel good, we have nevertheless made the contribution in both cases.

Chapter 9:
Other People's Problems Are Not Always Your Problems

A friend was telling me about how she was visiting a very close friend of hers. This friend was going through a tough time, and when my friend left, she felt this heavy weight on her. She felt a responsibility to make sure her friend was okay. She also felt inadequate because she couldn't solve her friend's problems. I told her, "You can't be responsible for another person's happiness."

This can be really hard at times, especially if you're a nurturing person or just deeply love the person who's struggling. You want to be the fixer. You want to help them find the solution, make smart choices and see the light.

It might even feel selfish NOT to intervene and take care of things. After all, aren't friends and loved ones supposed to support each other?

Yes, of course.

But there's a difference between loving and supporting someone and trying to fix their problems and make them happy. One you can do. The other you simply cannot. Everyone is responsible for their own happiness. And, in fact, trying to take on the responsibility of another person's happiness can hurt them in the long run and deprive them of miracles. When you feel the urge to be the fixer, follow the three steps I outline below. You'll feel immediate relief. You can release the need to be responsible for another person's happiness. The weight will be lifted and you'll be able to show up for your loved one AND yourself.

1. Everyone has their own guidance system, whatever it is they believe in — whether that's intuition, angels, spirit guides, the Universe or God. Even if they don't believe, there is a guidance that *we* believe in that we have to trust is protecting them and guiding them. Have faith in other people's guidance systems.

2. I learned this a long time ago. You don't want to deprive somebody of their bottom. Every one of us has experienced turning points in our lives. These are opportunities to pivot, to hit our knees and fully surrender. When you try to fix someone else, you just get in the way of their potential to experience this miracle. I want to encourage you to really own that you are not here to deprive anyone of their bottom. Give them the chance to experience exactly what they need to experience, and don't be afraid of it.

3. We have to be conscious of the fact that it's not our responsibility to change, or heal, or help, or resurrect anyone from their own issues and feelings. We have to trust that no one will change until they want to be changed. When they're ready for that change to come into their life, then you'll be there. You'll be able to show up for them when they're ready to show up for themselves.

The most loving thing we can do for someone is accept them for who they truly are. By consistently practicing to accept someone where they are and see them with compassion, you realign with your true love nature. Through acceptance you release the resistance you've placed within your relationship, clearing the way for healing and for you to access more loving thoughts and feelings. When you change your thoughts and feelings about another person, you change your energy toward them. The other person will receive your shift in energy and feel released by you. Best of all, your shift in energy gives you momentum to continue releasing judgment so you can feel complete and free. Acceptance offers you this freedom.

Chapter 10: How To Train Yourself to Be Optimistic and Positive

Positive thinking brings with it a whole host of benefits, such as better wellbeing and better sleep. To start reaping these benefits, check out how you can train your brain to be optimistic.

While many of us believe our happiness – or lack thereof – is based on external things, we're often the ones holding ourselves back. Many of us go through our days feeding ourselves negative messages we may not even be aware of, convincing ourselves we're "not good enough", "not clever enough" or "not attractive enough". To start thinking more positively, you need to change these messages. Try to look out for negative thoughts that pop into your head and replace them with positive messages. Write down some8 positive mantras and repeat them on a daily basis.

Most of us are happy to acknowledge other people's successes and accomplishments; however, when it comes to our own, we frequently play them down or ignore them entirely. To start thinking more positively about yourself, you need to regularly remind yourself of what you have – and can – achieve. Stop listening to your inner critic, reflect on your past achievements, and start to really appreciate your success and what you have to offer.

If you want to become an optimist, it can help to find yourself a positive role model. Whether it is a colleague, close friend or even a [celebrity](), think of the most unflappable, cheerful person you can. For the next few weeks, do an experiment and try to take a walk in their shoes. Whenever negativity starts creeping in or you find yourself in a difficult situation, think: "what would (insert name of chosen optimist) do?" Answer honestly, then try to follow suit.

It's important to remember that it isn't events themselves that make us unhappy, it is our interpretation and reaction to them, and while you can't always change events, you can change your response. When negative situations occur, try to reframe them by focusing on the positives or what you can learn from the situation. Maybe you have gained inner strength and resilience, grown closer to a friend through sharing your heartbreak or learned something about yourself. Try your best to focus on what you have learned and gained from your experience rather on than what you have lost.

When things don't go right in life, optimists tend to view each incident as an isolated event, while pessimists often look out for patterns of bad luck and think "if it happened once, it'll happen again". However, it is important not to try to predict the future based on what has happened before. Remember that a plan or relationship failing doesn't make you a failure and just because something disappointing has happened once (or more) it doesn't mean it will happen again.

What is [gone is gone](), and how you deal with the aftermath is the most important thing. There is no point apportioning blame, either on yourself or others. You have the power to change a situation and move on. It is so easy to say 'I should have done things differently' with the benefit of hindsight. However, if bad things have happened, look at tomorrow as exactly what it is — a new day — in which good things can happen, if you let them.

Chapter 11:
Why You Should Measure Everything

We, as a modern society, simply cannot live without measurement. The twenty-first-century civilization is unimaginable without the indispensable measurement tools on which our everyday life depends. Measurement permeates every aspect of our human lives. However, ironically, as much as it's crucial, we tend to take measures for granted. We fail to understand and appreciate how much we need and depend on these measurement tools. Another reason why we overlook the importance of measurement is because we have grown accustomed to it while being surrounded by it. We only realize their importance when they malfunction or are unavailable. Truly, we only know what we had when it's gone.

Imagine a normal day without any measurements; it sounds quite weird, right? You go to bed and wonder how, without any measurement like a clock or an alarm, would you wake up for work tomorrow? You won't be able to get awake at a selected time. But on the positive side, if there were no measures of time, then you, or anyone for that matter, can tell whether you were late for work or not. The very notion of being on time would vanish without any measurement.

After waking up, you could neither use an electric stove, oven, or microwave because these devices also rely on temperature measurements or time to heat food and beverages to a certain extent. Nor could you use a modern refrigerator since that too needs measurement of a preset temperature. You wouldn't be able to drive to work since an automobile requires measurement to control the ignition system, transmission, brakes, engine temperature, the mix of fuel and oxygen, etc., and you wouldn't be able to check the oil or fuel for your car without any measurement.

The things we measure are the things we improve. Through clear tracking of our measurement, we would get the idea of whether we're improving ourselves or getting worse. For example, if you start measuring how many pushups you do in one day, you'll eventually start doing more and get stronger. Similarly, if you track your reading habit of 15-20 pages per day, you would want to start reading more. When you measure your values and principles, you will start living with more integrity and honesty. Our lives are shaped by how much time and energy we spend each day. Measuring it can help us spend them in better and more consistent, and efficient ways.

Some things can't be measured in life. How much love do you give to a person, how much love you receive, how many moral values you have, how much meaning you find in your life? All these factors are immeasurable. Some things are better left unmeasured. For example, if a person is working out just for fun, measuring every repetition might reduce his satisfaction. It will start looking like a job instead. Measurement is not the ultimate answer to life; however, it is important to track something critical. The things we measure are the things we are most likely to improve. So, the question is, what are you measuring in life?

Chapter 12:
Why Getting Started Is More Important Than Succeeding

Our world is becoming more and more obsessed with comparison and validation. The style of thinking that is becoming dangerously common is "if you can't be number one or number two, then you might as well not play at all."

(this belief was celebrated in my mba program, which may or may not surprise you.)

But according to davenport, you don't need to be a professional to learn the most important lessons in sports. You just need to bust your butt as an athlete, regardless of the level you're playing at. I'd say it's that way in the rest of life as well. Mastering your craft isn't nearly as important as pushing yourself.

To put it another way, you'll learn more from the process of pursuing excellence than from the products of achieving it.

It's More Important To Start Than To Succeed

What if the choice to be curious was all that was required to become smarter, stronger, and more skilled? What if the willingness to try something new, even if it felt uncomfortable, was all that it took to start the slow march towards greatness?

- Are you curious enough to get in the gym and try it, even if you'll look stupid?

- Are you willing to be vulnerable and put your skin in the game to start your own business?

- Are you eager enough to improve your work that you'll battle through the frustration of producing something mediocre?

It all boils down to this: whether you'll end up being the best or the worst, are you willing to start?

The more i look at things this way, the more i believe that the willingness to start is the littlest thing in life that makes the biggest difference.

Step onto the field. Stand up in the meeting. Raise your hand in class.

Get under the bar. Walk up to the podium. Ask the first question.

Take a risk, get started, and contribute something. To your team, to your family, to your job, to your community. Whether or not you end up being number one in the world is irrelevant. Most of the time, the value you provide isn't nearly as important as pushing yourself to provide it. This is especially true at first.

Having the courage to get started is more important than succeeding because the people who consistently get started are the only ones who can end up finishing anything.

Get Started: Life Isn't A Dres's Rehearsal

I often write about what it means to live a healthy life.

I can't think of any skill more critical to the active pursuit of a healthy life than the willingness to start. Everything that signifies a happy, healthy and fulfilled existence — strong relationships, vibrant creativity, valuable work, a physical lifestyle, etc. — it all requires a willingness to get started over and over again.

Take note: being the best isn't required to be happy or fulfilled, but being in the game is necessary.

Life isn't a dress rehearsal. Only one person lives in the spotlight, but everyone benefits from stepping on stage.

Which stage will you step onto? What game will you play? How will you get started?

Chapter 13:
Why Nobody Cares When You Fail

In a world this big, it is hard for everyone to care about others. We all have a busy life; we have thousands of things to do before we go to bed. Everybody focuses on themselves and is trying to make their life better. So when anyone around us wins, their success makes the noise, and people notice that. Like when you sit in an interview, nobody will see how many times you have failed, but they will see that there is a reason that you are sitting in that interview.

The main reason why nobody cares if you fail is that everyone has a life of their own, and they can't just think or care about your failure for your whole life; sure, they would try to comfort you, but eventually, they will have to go back to their own lives, and they wouldn't care about your failure anymore, now they can't be blamed for this because it is simply human nature to resume their own lives.

People don't care about your failure, I mean, of course, your family and friends would, but others wouldn't because failures don't excite them; however insensitive it may sound to you, but it is the truth. People prefer to listen to success stories that excite them and, above all, motivate them.

The people themselves need someone to give them hope that one day they can also become a success, but nobody wants to care about failures; they would rather care about your success, so don't give up just yet because if they don't care now, they will care later. "Life is hard" we all have heard this, but this hits differently when we fail, but failures are not something to be afraid of; in this life, you can't always win; sometimes, you need to fail to gain success.

And honestly, what can people even do if you fail? Nobody can give you a happy and good life, and only you can make yourself a success. Failing is not a bad thing; it is something that no one can avoid, so when you fail, and you think that nobody cares, think for a second that maybe these people have also been through the same, and they know how it feels when people acknowledge your failures. People prefer to have a person they can call a hero, and they like to hear the stories of that hero and his success; even when the hero fails, nobody cares about his failure because they prefer to mind their own business when something like that happens.

Everyone is too focused on their own life, their own goals, and their failures to care about someone else's failures because they would rather care about their lives than yours, so don't take it negatively; it is okay if they don't care, use that to your advantage and work on yourself, now is the time to work hard and be successful and once your successful everyone will care.

The only thing you can do is forget about the people and remember yourself, remember that everyone who is a hero now has failed more than twice, so don't go thinking why they don't care because everyone has problems that they are worried about now and that is the reason they don't care. The only thing you should remember is that you should never give up because "Success comes from failures."

Chapter 14:
10 Life Skills That Men Need to Have

If you've made it far enough in life to be reading this, then you're already aware that you can't simply make it through life by existing. Not so long as you want to squeeze some real value out of the world around you or contribute in any kind of meaningful way. That being said, nobody is an expert on all things – even if they act like it. So long as you walk this Earth, there is always something to be learned. These are the 10 skills that every single man should know. So, man up and get schooled.

1. Basic Carpentry

Carpentry is one of humanity's oldest skills. Now, we're not suggesting that every man should be able to build a house from the ground up, but some general practices are definitely worth stashing away in your bank of skills. For example, knowing how to saw wood and use power tools, soundly nail or screw furniture together, and build something – even as basic as a single shelf – can come in handy if you ever want to be creative or helpful around the house.

2. Basic First Aid

Basic first aid is the most important survival skill to have in anyone's repertoire. Now, it's not something you're going to need every day –

or even every other day – but it can mean certain death if you don't have a grasp on how to clean and dress a wound when you need to.

3. Build A Campfire

Being able to build a proper campfire is an excellent skill to have whether you're in a survival situation or you just like to go camping now and again. The trick to building a good campfire is realizing that oxygen is an important part of fueling a flame. You can't simply light a stack of wood on fire. You need to give the fire room to breathe. You also need to know what kinds of wood to use (for instance, freshly cut branches will likely be too wet to burn) and that building a fire is sometimes a slow process when done right.

4. Build A Shelter

Hopefully you never find yourself in a situation where you need to sleep in the wilderness unexpectedly. But, if you do, you'll probably need to know how to put together a survival shelter. Not only will a simple structure help protect you from the elements – it'll also help ward off and/or keep you safe from wandering animals. Just remember: you're not just pitching a tent – you also need to pay attention to the area you're building in, because river beds, watering holes, and migration trails can all increase the area's danger.

5. Buy A Suit

You'd think that something like buying a suit would be as easy as walking into your local shop and asking for help. But, you'd be wrong. Buying a good suit is a lot more like buying a car than it is like purchasing casual apparel. Not only do you need to be able to differentiate styles based on for what you need it, but you also have to be able to discern between good deals and rip-offs. Furthermore, you'll want to get yourself sized by a reputable tailor beforehand and get the suit you choose trimmed to fit your body perfectly.

6. Catch A Fish

Fishing is an indispensable means by which to gather lean protein whether you're at the river, stuck on a desert island, or you just enjoy eating sushi. It's also a great way to kick back and relax during the nicer days of the year. There are also several means by which to catch a fish, so – if you can – see if you can pick up on a few of them and you'll be better off for it.

7. Change A Tire

Statistically speaking, you're going to end up with at least one flat tire in your lifetime if you drive a car daily. In the case that you do get a flat, you should know how to swap out the flat for the spare. It'll save you time waiting for someone else to come and help you – that is, if there's anyone coming at all. You see, if you get a flat out in the middle of nowhere, you'll probably be on your own. And you don't want to have to walk the rest of the way, do you?

8. Change Your Oil

If you don't regularly change your oil, your entire engine might break and it will be way more expensive to change. Pro tip: learning to change your own oil, while a bit more time consuming, is far cheaper than having a shop do it. Sure, you might not want to do it yourself all the time, but you can save some scratch and learn something valuable in the process if you take the time to do it yourself.

9. Compose A Photograph

Taking a good photo requires a lot more consideration than just aiming your camera and clicking. If you want to take the best shots, you have to consider everything from the position of the subject relative to the background, to depth of field, to lighting, and more. Even if you're just snapping photos for a family album.

10. Dress For The Occasion

Don't wear denim to a black-tie event. Don't wear a penguin tuxedo to a garden party. Don't wear your favorite band's tour t-shirt to a job interview. Sure, these seem like they go without saying, but they're extreme examples. Dressing properly for the occasion is a fine art and can sometimes require some guess and check, but it goes a long way to at least seem like you've got the right idea.

Chapter 15:
It's All About Networking

Networking isn't merely the exchange of information with others — and it's certainly not about begging for favors. Networking is about establishing and nurturing long-term, mutually beneficial relationships with the people you meet, whether you're waiting to order your morning coffee, participating in an intramural sports league, or attending a work conference. You don't have to join several professional associations and attend every networking event that comes your way in order to be a successful networker. In fact, if you take your eyes off your smartphone when you're out in public, you'll see that networking opportunities are all around you every day.

Experts agree that the most connected people are often the most successful. When you invest in your relationships — professional and personal — it can pay you back in dividends throughout the course of your career. Networking will help you develop and improve your skill set, stay on top of the latest trends in your industry, keep a pulse on the job market, meet prospective mentors, partners, and clients, and gain access to the necessary resources that will foster your career development.

Career development, in its simplest terms, is the lifelong evolution of your career. It's influenced by a number of things that include the jobs you hold, the experiences you gain in and out of the office, the success you achieve at each stage of your career, the formal and informal education and training you receive, and the feedback you're provided with along the way.

Ideally, organizations would place more emphasis on employee development in the workplace. However, the reality is that we live in what Carter Cast, author of the book, "The Right (and Wrong) Stuff: How Brilliant Careers Are Made," refers to as "the era of do-it-yourself career development."

Cast explains that in today's workforce, the burden is on you to take control of your career development. Hence the importance of networking for career development: As you network with people at your company, in your industry, and even outside your field of interest, you'll uncover opportunities to connect with different types of mentors and advisors, increase your visibility with senior management, further develop your areas of expertise, and improve your soft skills. You may assume that networking is an activity reserved for your time out of the office and off the clock, but nothing could be further from the truth. While there is much value in connecting with people who work at other companies or in different fields, don't discount the importance of networking in the workplace. Whether you're new to the company and want to get the lay of the land or you're already established and have your sights set on a promotion, networking with your co-workers can be incredibly beneficial to your career progression.

As you develop relationships with those in your department and in other divisions, be on the lookout for potential mentors, upcoming professional development opportunities, or new job opportunities that are not publicly advertised. It's never too early — or too late — to invest in your network. The best way to improve your networking skills is to put yourself out there and give it a try. According to Baikowitz, "the worst networking mistake you can make is not trying at all."

Chapter 16:
How To Develop An Incredible Work Ethic

We've all been there. That feeling of really, really not wanting to go into the office of a morning. It cripples productivity, raises stress levels, and makes us unhappy.

Why Do We Do It To Ourselves?

Unless it stems from deeper issues, the feeling of not wanting to go to work is often the result of a poor work ethic. If you've experienced it yourself recently, that doesn't make you a bad person or employee. A poor work ethic usually arrives subconsciously and is something you'll have little control over or forewarning of its impending arrival.

Thankfully, there are some methods you can employ to improve your work ethic dramatically, and they're not quite as tricky as you might think. To help you get out of that rut and back, fighting fit for a productive time in the office, we've decided to list our top eight tips for improving your work ethic.

1. Start With Your Body – Treat It Right

A healthy body will help you build a healthy approach to work because the two are intrinsically linked.

If you feel lethargic in the morning, the last thing you're going to want to do is to spring out of bed and head to the office. You're far more likely to continually hit the 'snooze' button and curse the fact you even have a job.

Lethargy can be a result of not enough sleep and poor levels of exercise. Therefore if the feeling just described is something you're all too familiar with, it's time to go on something of a permanent health kick. And that doesn't mean ditching all the treats that make you happy – just the process of regularly exercising and eating more healthily.

Walk when you'd normally take the car and swap those regular naughty treats for fruit and glasses of water – you'll be surprised how much more up for it you'll feel each morning.

2. Eliminate As Many Distractions As Possible

How many times do you check your email each day? What about social media? Is your facebook feed something you access every five minutes to check in on what your friends and family are up to?

We live in a world full of distractions. Multiple forms of content, relentless notifications and devices capable of connecting us immediately to the internet are everywhere and seemingly impossible to drag yourself away from.

That's true – unless you can call on your reserves of willpower. Distractions will divert your attention from what matters, and ensure that you have a limited focus on work tasks. In turn, that'll reduce your emotional connection with the business and negatively impact your work ethic.

Check your email only two or three times a day, turn off notifications and leave social media for the moments when you're sat on the sofa with nothing better to do.

3. Measure Your Ethic Against Others

If you're forever cursing your colleague's ability to practically skip into work ready for the day ahead, why not measure your performance against theirs?

Something is different. It might be their mindset, attitude towards their role or lifestyle, but if you can be brave enough to measure your performance against others, you'll quickly suss out where you need to improve.

This can extend far beyond work colleagues, too. For example, if your partner appears to be having the time of their life at work, yet you can barely muster the strength to log onto your computer for the first time each morning, ask them how they're doing it. You never know – you might just learn a thing or two.

Unless you're particularly spritely in the morning, it's unlikely that you'll jump out of bed and head to work full of an endless supply of energy. Still, if you follow our tips above, you'll greatly increase your ability to foster a healthy approach to work. Whenever you feel uninspired by your role, but you know it's something more superficial than job dissatisfaction, check that you're doing all you can to improve your work ethic. As we've demonstrated today, it isn't that difficult at all.

Chapter 17:
How To Stop Judging Your Own Work

Have you been extra nice to yourself lately? If you're a writer ... the answer is probably: "...mayyyybe?"

Writers — creators in general — are way too hard on themselves. We like making things, and we feel good doing it. But we really want to feel like we're doing a good job.

When we don't feel that way — which happens much more often than we realize — we start to doubt if writing is even worth the struggle.

Why are we so judgmental of our own work? Because it's the easiest to judge. It comes from us. We know it better than anyone.

But we can all learn to be critical without being so harsh. Here's how.

Remind yourself that not everything you write is going to feel polished. And the simple reason for that? The majority of the time, it won't be.

You have to make messes to make masterpieces. You have to do things wrong, you have to not do your best if you're ever going to learn what you're actually capable of. If what you're writing seems terrible — well, it might be. That doesn't mean it always will be, or that it will be the best thing you'll ever write.

You're going to write sentences you're unsure of, paragraphs that just don't "sound quite right." You're going to question whether or not this scene should stay or go. You're going to ask yourself a million times if you're doing any of this right.

What matters most is that you keep writing anyway. You can't polish something unfinished. Even if a draft feels like the worst thing you've ever written, at least you have something to work with — something you can improve little by little until it meets your personal standards (if that's even possible …).

Focus on how you feel about your work, not on how others might react. We're all guilty of imagining how our future readers will react to certain parts of our stories. Sometimes, it's what keeps you going when you're starting to feel unsure. When you laugh at your own writing (admit it — it happens to you too), you picture others laughing too.

But there's a dark side to this train of thought. If we focus too much on what people might think about our writing, we can begin to worry that they won't like it. That they'll tell everyone else not to read it. That our words aren't actually good … that they never will be.

The best way to judge whether or not your writing is meaningful and readable is if it feels that way to you. Yes, your readers matter whether they exist yet or not. You are writing for their entertainment. But until you get your words in front of eyes, the only opinion that matters is yours.

Your inner critic will never stop talking, but you can tune it out. Here's the truth not every writing expert will tell you: you will never stop doubting or judging yourself or your writing. There is no magic cure for self-criticism. But that doesn't mean you can't tone it down enough to avoid letting it interfere with your work.

We judge ourselves more harshly than everyone else does (even though it sometimes feels the other way around) because we genuinely want to do a good job. And deep down we know we are the only ones in control of whether or not we do the work "well."

The problem is, we're so used to seeing others' work and the kinds of writing that gets high praise that we often can't help but compare our drafts to their published masterpieces. When we do that, our writing just never feels "as good." We immediately spiral into "i'll never be good enough" self-talk. We get sad. We stop writing.

That negative self-talk will always be there. You will always hear it.

But you don't have to listen to it.

You don't have to care about the lies it's telling you. You don't have to let them stop you from doing the work you know you're meant to do.

It's one thing to say you're not going to pay attention to your voice of doubt and another to actually ignore it. It's not that simple for a lot of people — and that's ok. Some have an easier time quieting their minds than others. As a writer, it's often one of those things you learn to do the longer you do it, the more you practice it.

That voice in your head telling you that you'll never achieve your dreams?

The best thing you can do to demote its scream to a whisper is to prove it wrong.

Chapter 18:
3 Steps To Choose Mind Over Mood

Have you ever said something out of anger that you later regretted? Do you let fear talk you out of taking the risks that could really benefit you? If so, you're not alone.

Emotions are powerful. Your mood determines how you interact with people, how much money you spend, how you deal with challenges, and how you spend your time.

Gaining control over your emotions will help you become mentally stronger. Fortunately, anyone can become better at choosing their mind over their mood. Just like any other skill, managing your emotions requires practice and dedication. Managing your emotions isn't the same as suppressing them. Ignoring your sadness or pretending you don't feel pain won't make those emotions go away.

In fact, unaddressed emotional wounds are likely to get worse over time. And there's a good chance suppressing your feelings will cause you to turn to unhealthy coping skills--like food or alcohol. It's important to acknowledge your feelings while also recognizing that your emotions don't have to control you. If you wake up on the wrong side of the bed, you can take control of your mood and turn your day around. If you are angry, you can choose to calm yourself down.

Here are three ways to gain better control over your mood:

1. Label Your Emotions

Before you can change how you feel, you need to acknowledge what you're experiencing right now. Are you nervous? Do you feel disappointed? Are you sad?

Keep in mind that anger sometimes masks emotions that feel vulnerable--like shame or embarrassment. So pay close attention to what's really going on inside of you.

Put a name your emotions. Keep in mind you might feel a whole bunch of emotions at once--like anxious, frustrated, and impatient.

Labeling how you feel can take a lot of the sting out of the emotion. It can also help you take careful note of how those feelings are likely to affect your decisions.

2. Reframe Your Thoughts

Your emotions affect the way you perceive events. If you're feeling anxious and you get an email from the boss that says she wants to see you right away, you might assume you're going to get fired. If however, you're feeling happy when you get that same email, your first thought might be that you're going to be promoted or congratulated on a job well done.

Consider the emotional filter you're looking at the world through. Then, reframe your thoughts to develop a more realistic view.

If you catch yourself thinking, "This networking event is going to be a complete waste of time. No one is going to talk to me and I'm going to look like an idiot," remind yourself, "It's up to me to get something out of the event. I'll introduce myself to new people and show interest in learning about them."

Sometimes, the easiest way to gain a different perspective is to take a step back and ask yourself, "What would I say to a friend who had this problem?" Answering that question will take some of the emotion out of the equation so you can think more rationally.

If you find yourself dwelling on negative things, you may need to change the channel in your brain. A quick physical activity, like going for a walk or cleaning off your desk, can help you stop ruminating.

3. Engage in a Mood Booster

When you're in a bad mood, you're likely to engage in activities that keep you in that state of mind. Isolating yourself, mindlessly scrolling through your phone, or complaining to people around you are just a few of the typical "go-to bad mood behaviors" you might indulge in.

But, those things will keep you stuck. You have to take positive action if you want to feel better.

Think of the things you do when you feel happy. Do those things when you're in a bad mood and you'll start to feel better.

Here are a few examples of mood boosters:

- Call a friend to talk about something pleasant (not to continue complaining).
- Go for a walk.
- Meditate for a few minutes.
- Listen to uplifting music.

Keep Practicing Your Emotional Regulation Skills

Managing your emotions is tough at times. And there will likely be a specific emotion--like anger--that sometimes gets the best of you.

But the more time and attention you spend on regulating your emotions, the mentally stronger you'll become. You'll gain confidence in your ability to handle discomfort while also knowing that you can make healthy choices that shift your mood.

Chapter 19:
8 Ways To Turn Stress Into Strength

We tend to think of stress as all bad, but it doesn't have to be. Without stress, we might feel less motivated, and if we're pushing our life forward, getting things done and achieving our goals, stress will always be part of that. Stress is a fixed and natural part of our lives so, instead of trying to fight it or get rid of it, we need to make stress work for us by learning how to manage it better. Here are 10 ways you can manage your stress and make it work for you

1.Build a 'stress wall'

During stressful periods, you might feel bombarded by stressful thoughts that trigger anxiety. When a thought comes, try using active imagination to combat it. Imagine the worry bouncing off a big impenetrable wall in your mind and floating away from your immediate attention. Keep that wall up until you're ready to deal with the problem, and imagine all the further stressful thoughts continuing to bounce off it. When you stop allowing stressful thoughts to permeate your mind, you'll be able to manage stress a lot more effectively.

You don't have to imagine a wall - you can choose any thought metaphor that suits you. You might prefer to imagine your thoughts as birds landing on a tree and you make them fly away again or putting your thoughts into a box and closing the lid.

2. Stop living in the world of what if

When we're stressed, we live in the world of what if.

What if this happens?... What if I can't do that?... What if I make a fool out of myself?

Most of these worrying thoughts never happen, and they're only getting in your way. Try to stop living in the world of what if and start living in the land of the real. So what if something doesn't go quite right? You've just learned something new, and there is always value in that. Don't be afraid to take a chance.

3. Focus on positive people

Where your lifestyle allows it, try to spend more time with people who will have a positive influence on your wellbeing. This doesn't necessarily mean people who don't get as stressed as you - in fact someone who is going through the same emotions as you could act as a buddy and you could help each other to be more productive with your stress management.

4. Learn to let go

If you have a heavy workload or money/relationship worries, it makes you feel out of control. Feeling out of control causes stress. The more we fight to control a situation the more stressed it makes us. Accept that it's not possible to control every situation in life. Unclench your fists, lower your shoulders and stop screwing up your face. Take a breath and let it go - for instant stress relief.

5. Set a deadline

Parkinson's law says "work expands so as to fill the time available for its completion". In other words, if you set a deadline you're more likely to get a task done within that timescale. By not having a deadline, you're risking living a life filled with unfinished business. That's only going to lead to one thing: stress! Set a deadline on every task that comes up in your life and watch how much more you get done.

6. Be present and mindful

Stress is usually related to our past and future – worrying about what we've done and what we need to do. Take a second to appreciate this moment, right now. The more often you can live in the present the less stressed you're going to be. The past is over, and the future hasn't happened yet. Are they really worth all that worry?

7. Focus on what you want

Whatever you focus on, and put more energy into, you're going to get more of it in your life. Focus on being stressed, and there are no prizes for guessing what you'll get in return. Try focusing on what it is you want, and you'll naturally gravitate in that direction. Write down your targets and goals right now, and make those your focus.

8. Be grateful

Lack of gratitude breeds stressful thoughts and feelings. Practice being grateful for what you have, rather than worrying about what you don't have. Think about five things you can be grateful for right now. Take five every day and practice being more grateful.

You should also sometimes feel grateful for your feelings of stress as, without them, feeling relaxed wouldn't be as satisfying.

Chapter 20:
How To Spend Money Wisely

Financial struggles could be of many types, I.E., Not bringing in enough money, not spending money wisely, or simply spending more money than making. According to time, nearly 73% of Americans die in debt. Sure, we're guilty of slipping up at one point or the other. It's quite easy to fall into the habit of buying expensive coffee every day, eating out or ordering takeaways, and getting our hands on groceries that we have eventually ended up throwing out. We don't have to be an expert in personal finances nor have A big investment portfolio to be financially secure. It is, however, essential to understand the basics of financial planning.

Before you can start figuring out how to spend your money wisely, you need to analyse and understand where exactly your money is going. Make A budget to track both your expenses and your income. Once you get your hands on where the money is going, you can start looking for better opportunities where they could be spent instead.

Need I tell you that far too many purchases are impulse decisions? It can be fine on A shorter scale, like buying A $1 chocolate, but it can become

A serious problem for larger purchases. Before you buy something, think about A few factors first; like how it's going to affect you in the future, how long is it going to last, is it going to put you in debt, is the value you will get out of it over its lifetime worth the cost. These are the questions that you really should ask yourself to determine if the product is worth buying or are you only satisfying your inner cravings.

The average person spends far too much money in trying to maintain an image in front of others. Fancy cars, brand-name clothing, expensive watches, and perfumes, all these that we buy have more to do with impressing others than it does with purchasing something that we want to enjoy. This pursuit is far too expensive and unnecessary. Buy the things that you enjoy yourself and never fall prey to the feeling that you have to spend your money in bulk to impress people.

After you have started to track your finances, you can keep an eye on the habits that may be draining your budget. These habits could include expensive hobbies, eating out too much, stress shopping, spending loads of money on your friends/partner, or any number of other financial drains. Once you have figured out which habits are eating up large portions of your income, you can then self-evaluate whether these habits are actually worth your money or not.

Some people are naturally good at saving money. They draw enjoyment from growing their wealth. While for others, money is something that is spent the moment it reaches their hands. Anything else feels like A wasted opportunity for them. If you find yourself falling in the latter category, try and adopt A mentality that values savings over products. In the end, money spent on products that will wear or become uninteresting will always be lesser than money invested or money saved that will always benefit you.

Spending your money wisely isn't always about just avoiding unnecessary purchases - it also requires you to take the money that you save and put it towards your financial goals. With that in mind, it's never going to be about starting investing too early or too late. No matter how young or old you are, invest your money in things that will benefit you. Your spent money growing in value as time goes on is always A wise use of it.

Chapter 21:
6 Ways To Get More Attention

In my mind, there are two kinds of attention: neck down, and neck up. Neck-up attention is when the listener has to make an effort to pay attention. Neck-down attention is when the listener is riveted to the speaker: she can't help but pay attention.

Please note that, in our language of English, attention is *paid* because attention is a valuable currency. When listeners *pay* attention, they are rewarding you with arguably the most valuable currency in the world. Here are 6 techniques that are guaranteed to earn you more attention without losing any of your professional credibility.

1. Start with the unexpected

Start with a bang, not a whimper. Smokers like matches that light with the first strike, and listeners like presentations that ignite interest with the first sentence. For instance:

"We stand today at a place of battle, one that 40 years ago saw and felt the worst of war."--President Ronald Reagan

These kind of opening lines make us lean in, lend an ear, and wonder where the speaker will take us. They jump right into the subject and create suspense, intrigue, curiosity. They capture *neck-down* attention.

2. Make it about them

Now that you've gotten listeners' attention with your magnetic opening, make the story about them. Increase your You-to-Me-Ratio. Talk about *their* goals, *their* aspirations, *their* anxieties. Cicero, a Roman statesman and orator, and one of the greatest speakers in the history of the world, said, "Tickling and soothing anxieties is the test of a speaker's impact and technique." He meant that you can capture attention if you remind an audience of a felt need, a pain point, or a threat to their well-being.

"Ring around the collar," was a 1968 ad in which a housewife protected her husband from loss of social status and career disaster by using Whisk on his shirts. And many consultants I know use something called FUD to sell their projects: Fear, Uncertainty, and Doubt. A smattering of FUD gets our attention. When I feel it, I feel it in my chest.

3. Keep it concrete at the start

Show a prop. Use language that appeals to the senses. Don't tax the audience right away with abstract reasoning or academic concepts. Better to hide your smarts than to wear them on your sleeve. Storytelling is a powerful way to get into a topic because we are hard-wired to absorb information through storytelling. Tell a good story and you'll get neck-down attention.

I once heard Robert Kennedy, Jr. speak about conservation on a boat on the Hudson River. He began by pointing south. "If you look in that direction," he said, "You will see the channel that for millions of years has been the largest spawning ground for sturgeon in the world."

Of course, when I looked where he was pointing, I saw nothing but gray polluted water, not a sturgeon in sight, but I had the image of millions of large fish teeming so densely on the surface of the river that I could have walked across their backs to New Jersey.

Only then did he dive into the data about the poor, languishing Hudson.

4. Keep it moving

Not just in terms of pace, but in terms of development. Make sure that every new bit of information you provide builds on what came before. We lose interest in movies when nothing is happening, or novels that stop while the author describes a bucolic setting for two pages. Our brains are saying, "I want action! Drama. Suspense." The same holds true for your listeners. They are time-pressed, content-driven, and results oriented.

Think of the difference between a river and a canal. A canal is plodding while a river is dynamic and constantly changing. To please your listeners' insatiable desire for *variety,* make your presentations like rivers, not canals. Make sure there's always something happening, most especially when delivering webinars, where your audience is likely to be highly distracted.

it early and often, and they'll carry you out on their shoulders.

5. Write clear headlines

Write headlines for your slides that express a point of view. The audience will get the big idea and look at the body of the slide for evidence that supports your point.

For instance, "We Can Dominate the Market" is a better headline than, "Market Share." It's better because it implies *action*, it's brimming with intellectual and emotional *content*, and it captures the physicality of neck-down attention much more than the inert phrase "Market Share."

6. Keep it short

Stop talking before they stop listening. The mind cannot absorb what the behind cannot endure.

Chapter 22:
9 Tips To Reduce Stress

Stress and anxiety are common experiences for most people. In fact, 70% of adults in the United States say they feel stress or anxiety daily. Here are 16 simple ways to relieve stress and anxiety.

1. Exercise

Exercise is one of the most important things you can do to combat stress. It might seem contradictory, but putting physical stress on your body through exercise can relieve mental stress. The benefits are strongest when you exercise regularly. People who exercise regularly are less likely to experience anxiety than those who don't exercise. Activities such as walking or jogging that involve repetitive movements of large muscle groups can be particularly stress relieving.

2. Consider supplements

Several supplements promote stress and anxiety reduction. Here is a brief overview of some of the most common ones:

Lemon balm: Lemon balm is a member of the mint family that has been studied for its anti-anxiety effects.

Omega-3 fatty acids: One study showed that medical students who received omega-3 supplements experienced a 20% reduction in anxiety symptoms.

Ashwagandha: Ashwagandha is an herb used in Ayurvedic medicine to treat stress and anxiety. Several studies suggest that it's effective.

Green tea: Green tea contains many polyphenol antioxidants which provide health benefits. It may lower stress and anxiety by increasing serotonin levels.

Valerian: Valerian root is a popular sleep aid due to its tranquilizing effect. It contains valerenic acid, which alters gamma-aminobutyric acid (GABA) receptors to lower anxiety.

Some supplements can interact with medications or have side effects, so you may want to consult with a doctor if you have a medical condition.

3. Light a candle

Using essential oils or burning a scented candle may help reduce your feelings of stress and anxiety.

Some scents are especially soothing. Here are some of the most calming scents:

- Lavender
- Rose
- Vetiver
- Bergamot
- Roman chamomile
- Neroli
- Frankincense
- Orange or orange blossom
- Geranium

Using scents to treat your mood is called aromatherapy. Several studies show that aromatherapy can decrease anxiety and improve sleep.

4. Reduce your caffeine intake

Caffeine is a stimulant found in coffee, tea, chocolate and energy drinks. High doses can increase anxiety. People have different thresholds for how much caffeine they can tolerate. If you notice that caffeine makes you jittery or anxious, consider cutting back. Although many studies show that coffee can be healthy in moderation, it's not for everyone. In general, five or fewer cups per day is considered a moderate amount.

5. Write it down

One way to handle stress is to write things down. While recording what you're stressed about is one approach, another is jotting down what you're grateful for. Gratitude may help relieve stress and anxiety by focusing your thoughts on what's positive in your life.

6. Chew gum

For a super easy and quick stress reliever, try chewing a stick of gum. One study showed that people who chewed gum had a greater sense of wellbeing and lower stress. One possible explanation is that chewing gum causes brain waves similar to those of relaxed people. Another is that chewing gum promotes blood flow to your brain. Additionally, one recent study found that stress relief was greatest when people chewed more strongly.

7. Spend time with friends and family

Social support from friends and family can help you get through stressful times. Being part of a friend network gives you a sense of belonging and self-worth, which can help you in tough times. One study found that for women in particular, spending time with friends and children helps release oxytocin, a natural stress reliever. This effect is called "tend and befriend," and is the opposite of the fight-or-flight response. Keep in mind that both men and women benefit from friendship. Another study found that men and women with the fewest social connections were more likely to suffer from depression and anxiety.

8. Laugh

It's hard to feel anxious when you're laughing. It's good for your health, and there are a few ways it may help relieve stress: Relieving your stress response. Relieving tension by relaxing your muscles.
In the long term, laughter can also help improve your immune system and mood. A study among people with cancer found that people in the laughter intervention group experienced more stress relief than those who were simply distracted. Try watching a funny TV show or hanging out with friends who make you laugh.

9. Learn to say no

Try not to take on more than you can handle. Saying no is one way to control your stressors.

Chapter 23:
When It Is Time To Slow Down

Go faster. Do more. Hustle. Hustle even more. Sound familiar? Social media is full of influencers, entrepreneurs, and "gurus" touting the virtues of hustling at all costs. It's reached the point where hustling, and even just talking about hustling, appears to be more important that actually producing results. People confuse "hustling" with "productivity" and mistake "working" for "results." They don't have a mindfulness practice. They didn't make time for trips, fun, friends, or family. They think that if they worked harder, and worked more hours, they'd be more successful. That is not true if all you do is work, work work. You will be burnt out.

The antidote to the "always hustling" mindset is "slowness." It sounds crazy, but slowing down can be the difference between success or failure, or between thriving and burning out. While more and more personal coaches and social-media influencers, qualified or not, tout the hustle lifestyle, successful leaders and entrepreneurs who actually create results in their lives know that slowing down builds the foundation for their success. Here are four reasons why slowing down can actually help you accelerate your success, enjoy a deeper sense of fulfillment, and create the life you want.

1. What's the point of hustling if you're going in the wrong direction? Too many people work tirelessly down a path that won't give them the results they want. It's like running on a treadmill...you're working, but you're not going anywhere. Slow

down and make time for clarity. You can't see where you're going if you're too busy running with your head down.

2. If your goal is to succeed, then you should be willing to take the time to honor what your mind, body, and spirit need to stay healthy. When every day provides 24 hours, there's really no excuse not to meditate, exercise, cook a healthy meal, or journal.

3. Too many people fail to see the benefits in their emotions. Emotions are a guide, and they help you take inventory of what's happening in and around you, and how best to respond. Successful people feel and manage their emotions, and they don't let them trigger bad behaviors or actions. There's a mantra that sums this up well: If you can name it, you can tame it. By slowing down, you can feel the emotions you're experiencing and describe them. In doing so, you can process them and let them guide you to a healthy response.

4. What good is hustling all the time if a single decision can undo all the work you invested? To put it simply, your mind is like a car engine: If you always have your pedal to the floor, the engine will redline, overheat, and fail. When you slow down and make time for rest and meditation, you lower your baseline for mental stress. When your mind isn't racing, it's free to absorb information, assess the circumstances, and make a good decision. If success requires making good decisions, and slowing down helps you make better decisions, then consider how you can invest more time in slowing down.

Consider the benefits described above and identify one simple step toward bringing more slowness into your life. See how that goes, and then try more. As someone who hustled himself into a concussion and changed, I can tell you that life is much better when you balance the hustle with slowness.

Chapter 24:
10 Work From Home Hacks

As good as it is working from home and being your own boss, so to speak, there are still plenty of obstacles to navigate while working remotely, including the warm, comforting embrace of your old friend the television. Well, turn it off and get to work, because here are 10 tips to ensure you become a remote working legend.

1. Walk or run around the block before work

It's all very well and good having the shortest commute of all time, but an active commute has been shown to enhance performance and keep blood, glucose and oxygen levels high — so try leaving the house for a brisk 15-minute run or walk before opening the laptop. As well as providing a cognitive boost, it gives you an excuse to get dressed properly, ensuring you're less likely to fall into any bad habits than you would do in your PJs.

2. Break work up into 25-minute chunks

One of the biggest benefits of not working in an office is being able to buck the herd mentality and work to your own beat. The Pomodoro Method – a time management system breaking down work into 25 minute spells separated by short breaks of between 3 and 5 minutes – is a perfect way to help dice up your day. Scientifically proven to increase your output.

3. Find your ultradian rhythm

Want to achieve the heightened state known as 'flow', which, according to many leading neuroscientists, leaves you more receptive to activity immersion and miles more productive? Well, pay attention to the times you feel productive in a day. The brain cycles through 90-minute periods of extreme efficiency, known as ultradian cycles, when your mind is where you're more attuned than ever. The cycle in which we dip in and out of them is called the ultradian rhythm - tap into yours and you'll be a remote working dynamo.

4. Utilise Gmail's scheduling tool

Even if you do start early and smash all your targets by 4 pm, one of the pitfalls of working from home is having to maintain the illusion that you're always present, always on. So thank the lord of early finishes, then, for Gmail, which you may not have realised features a scheduling tool allowing you to fire off emails at pre-set times. Simply compose an email, click the blue button with a triangle icon next to 'send', schedule exactly when you want a message to leave your outbox.

5. Spend time with a pet

It may sound counterintuitive but playing with your pooch may help you smash through your workload while working from home (WFH). Pet owners are also less likely to suffer from loneliness, so if you don't already own a furry colleague, it might be the best time to take one home.

6. Invest in a stand-up desk

Just as in an office, being hunched over a table all day isn't going to be all that good for your back, and before you say it, lying on the sofa isn't going to make you all that productive, either. The answer? A mini standup desk, giving you the opportunity to mix it up when you fancy a change of scenery and improve your focus.

7. Journal like a pro

One surefire way to keep on top of your workload is with a digital To-Do List. Streamline your thoughts, ideas and tasks in one place, even using photos, videos, drawings, or audio recordings to bring your journal entries to life.

8. Use a different browser for work

Procrastinationville, population: you. Despite best-laid plans, with social media and the hum of 24hour rolling news, it's all too easy to end up here when you don't have the boss's eyes on you. One surefire way to keep focused is to have one browser, i.e Google Chrome, specifically for work-related bits. Bookmarks, tabs, shortcuts, plugins - make them all work-related and you'll be distraction-free in no time. Trust us, it works.

9. Make your workspace green

Numerous scientific studies have proven that plants in the workplace can increase product productivity among employees. If nothing else, they'll also help make your environment look a bit more swish.

10. Turn the music off occasionally

The jury may still be out on whether music at work is a help or a hindrance, but at least where creative thinking is concerned at least, experts are largely in agreement that background music can stifle creativity. That's not to say you shouldn't listen to music while you are really up against it, best pause that Spotify playlist and tune in to your inner voice.

Chapter 25:
6 Ways To Master Your Emotions

As reported by Psychology Today, psychology's answer to the question of "What is emotional mastery?" Has evolved over the last century. Early American psychology embraced the "James-Lange Theory," which held that emotions are strictly the product of physiology (a neurological response to some external stimuli). This view evolved when the "Cannon-Bard Theory" asserted that the brain's thalamus mediates between external stimuli and subjective emotional experience.

The concept of emotional mastery wasn't introduced until the 1960s with the Schachter-Singer experiment, where researchers gave participants a dose of a placebo "vitamin." Participants then watched colleagues complete a set of questionnaires. When the colleagues responded angrily to the questionnaires, the participants felt angry in turn. But when the colleagues responded happily, the participants also felt happy. The study's results implied a connection between peer influence and the felt experience of emotion.

The idea that emotions are influenced by outer as well as inner stimuli was furthered by psychiatrist Allen Beck, who demonstrated that thoughts, peer influence and circumstance shape emotions. Beck's research formed the foundation of modern-day cognitive-behavioral therapy, the gold standard of emotional mastery as it's understood today.

The Role Of Emotional Mastery In Life And Society

Feelings and emotional mastery play a role in our subjective experience and interpersonal relationships.

- **Emotions unify us across cultural lines.** There are six basic emotions that are universal in all cultures: happiness, sadness, fear, anger, surprise and disgust. We all experience these feelings, although there are cultural differences regarding what's an appropriate display of emotion.

- **Emotions govern our sense of well-being.** Since emotions are a product of our experiences and how we perceive those experiences, we can cultivate positive emotions by focusing on them. There are 10 "power emotions" that cultivate emotional mastery by creating a base of positive affect. When we incorporate even small doses of gratitude, passion, love, hunger, curiosity, confidence, flexibility, cheerfulness, vitality and a sense of contribution, we set the stage for feeling good about ourselves.

- **Emotional mastery supports healthy relationships.** When you're able to demonstrate emotions that are appropriate to the situation, you're able to nurture your relationships. When you don't know how to master your emotions, the opposite occurs: You might fly off the handle at minor annoyances or react with anger when sadness is a more appropriate response. Your emotional response affects those around you, which shapes your relationships for better or worse.

Learning how to master your emotions is a skill anyone can build in six straightforward steps.

1. Identify what you're really feeling

The first step in learning how to master your emotions is identifying what your feelings are. To take that step toward emotional mastery, ask yourself:

- What am i really feeling right now?
- Am i really feeling…?
- Is it something else?
-

2. Acknowledge and appreciate your emotions, knowing they support you

Emotional mastery does not mean shutting down or denying your feelings. Instead, learning how to master your emotions means appreciating them as part of yourself.

- You never want to make your emotions wrong.
- The idea that anything you feel is "wrong" is a great way to destroy honest communication with yourself as well as with others.

3. Get curious about the message this emotion is offering you

Emotional mastery means approaching your feelings with a sense of curiosity. Your feelings will teach you a lot about yourself if you let them. Getting curious helps you:

- Interrupt your current emotional pattern.
- Solve the challenge.
- Prevent the same problem from occurring in the future.
-

4. Get confident

The quickest and most powerful route to emotional mastery over any feeling is to remember a time when you felt a similar emotion and handled it successfully. Since you managed the emotion in the past, surely you can handle it today.

5. Get certain you can handle this not only today, but in the future as well

To master your emotions, build confidence by rehearsing handling situations where this emotion might come up in the future. See, hear and feel yourself handling the situation. This is the equivalent of lifting emotional weights, so you'll build the "muscle" you need to handle your feelings successfully.

5. Get excited and take action

Now that you've learned how to master your emotions, it's time to get excited about the fact that you can:

- Easily handle this emotion.
- Take some action right away.
- Prove that you've handled it.

Learning emotional mastery is one of the most powerful steps you can take to create a life that's authentic and fulfilling.

Chapter 26:
3 Ways To Master Your Next Move

"I don't know what to do with my life!" If you find yourself saying this, you're not alone. It's common for people to get to a point where they feel stuck or directionless. It can result from poor decision making or an inability to make decisions at all.

This state of not knowing what to do next applies to a lot of people, at any age and at different times in your life.

Personally, I have discovered that following these 5 steps will help you to find out what to do with your life, feel good, and get unstuck.

1. Get Moving and Clear Your Mind

"Not knowing what you want is a lot better than knowing exactly what you want but not being able to get it, at least you have hope."

I once faced a very challenging and emotional time; all I could do was think about what I needed to do to get to the next day.

There were no thoughts of what I wanted to do in the future nor were there any thoughts of how I wanted my life to be. It was just a matter of surviving from one day to the next.

For me, during this challenging time, when I was telling myself, "I don't know what to do with my life," exercise was the solution to helping me get through my day.

Every morning my alarm would go off at 6 am. I would have my running gear ready by the bed. I would get dressed, walk out the door, and start running for 45 minutes.

For a long time, it was hard to get out of bed and go for my run because I just wanted to hide away. Over time, I began to look forward to my morning run as I felt more energized, and I was sleeping better.

2. Wake Your Conscious Mind and Limit Choices

"Nobody is going to do your life for you. You have to do it yourself, whether you're rich or poor, out of money or making it, the beneficiary of ridiculous fortune or terrible injustice…Self pity is a dead end road. You can make the choice to drive down it. It's up to you to decide to stay parked there or to turn around and drive out." -Cheryl Stryed.

Life isn't predictable, and the solutions we seek to answer our life questions don't always come nicely wrapped. There are no rules to follow, and you have to work hard to define your life pathway when you don't know what to do with your life.

Waking our conscious minds to accept our reality and embrace change is one step toward finding out what we need to do next in our life.

We become paralyzed rather than liberated by the power of choice. When we are presented with too many options, our brain doesn't know what to do with it all.

Research has shown that there is a sweet spot when it comes to choices. If we have too few, we feel limited. If we have too many, we feel overwhelmed.

How does this translate to your everyday life? If you're changing career fields and aren't sure what to switch over to, limit your options to five or six possible areas. Choose to mark one off the list every few days once you've sat with the choices a bit. As your brain focuses on fewer and fewer choices, it will become easier to see the direction you genuinely want to go in.

3. Take Small Steps With a 30-Day Challenge

In order to reprogram your conscious mind and stop saying "I don't know what to do with my life," set yourself a 30-day challenge.

You may ask, why 30 days? Because this is how the small steps you take gradually become your powerful habits

Setting a deadline has a powerful effect on motivation. Research has shown time and again that deadlines, even those that are self-imposed, can reduce procrastination and lead to better decision making.

Try setting one to three goals to be achieved during your 30-day challenge. Maybe you want to learn to code. Set weekly goals related to free online courses, and by the end of the month you'll have a good deal of knowledge under your belt.

Or perhaps you want to spend more time with your kids. Make a goal to have one family night each week where you offer all of your attention to your kids. You can even let them help plan what you will do on that special night.

Achieving these goals after one month will give you the confidence and self belief to keep going. It also helps you avoid doing nothing while you're feeling stuck. Once you know you can achieve one goal, you'll go on to achieve more and more.

Chapter 27:
3 Ways To Calm The Emotional Storm Within You

When emotions are already intense, it's often hard to think about what you can do to help yourself, so the first thing you need to work on is getting re-regulated as quickly as possible. Here are some fast-acting skills that work by changing your body's chemistry; it will be most helpful if you first try these before you're in an emotional situation, so you know how to use them.

1. Do a forward bend

This is my favourite re-regulating skill. Bend over as though you're trying to touch your toes (it doesn't matter if you can actually touch your toes; you can also do this sitting down if you need to, by sticking your head between your knees). Take some slow, deep breaths, and hang out there for a little while (30 to 60 seconds if you can). Doing a forward bend actually activates our parasympathetic nervous system – our 'rest and digest' system – which helps us slow down and feel a little calmer. When you're ready to stand up again, just don't do it too quickly – you don't want to fall over.

2. Focus on your exhale with 'paced breathing'

It might sound like a cliché but breathing truly is one of the best ways to get your emotions to a more manageable level. In particular, focus on making your exhale longer than your inhale – this also activates our parasympathetic nervous system, again helping us feel a little calmer and getting those emotions back to a more manageable level. When you inhale, count in your head to see how long your inhale is; as you exhale, count at the same pace, ensuring your exhale is at least a little bit longer than your inhale. For example, if you get to 4 when you inhale, make sure you exhale to at least 5. For a double whammy, do this breathing while doing your forward bend.

These re-regulating skills will help you to think a little more clearly for a few minutes, but your emotions will start to intensify once more if nothing else has changed in your environment – so the next steps are needed too.

3. Increase awareness of your emotions

In order to manage emotions more effectively in the long run, you need to be more aware of your emotions and of all their components; and you need to learn to name your emotions accurately. This might sound strange – of course you know what you're feeling, right? But how do you know if what you've always called 'anger' is actually anger, and not anxiety? Most of us have never really given our emotions much thought, we just assume that what we think we feel is what we actually feel – just like we assume the colour we've always called 'blue' is actually blue; but how do we really know?

Sensitive people who have grown up in a pervasively invalidating environment often learn to ignore or not trust their emotional experiences, and try to avoid or escape those experiences, which contributes to difficulties naming emotions accurately. Indeed, anyone prone to emotion dysregulation can have trouble figuring out what they're feeling, and so walks around in an emotional 'fog'. When you're feeling 'upset', 'bad' or 'off', are you able to identify what emotion you're actually feeling? If you struggle with this, consider each of the following questions the next time you experience even a mild emotion:

- What was the prompting event or trigger for the feeling? What were you reacting to? (Don't judge whether your response was right or wrong, just be descriptive.)

- What were your thoughts about the situation? How did you interpret what was happening? Did you notice yourself judging, jumping to conclusions, or making assumptions?

- What did you notice in your body? For example, tension or tightness in certain areas? Changes in your breathing, your heart rate, your temperature?

- What was your body doing? Describe your body language, posture and facial expression.

- What urges were you noticing? Did you want to yell or throw things? Was the urge to not make eye contact, to avoid or escape a situation you were in?

- What were your actions? Did you act on any of the urges you noted above? Did you do something else instead?

Going through this exercise will help you increase your ability to name your emotions accurately. Once you've asked yourself the above questions, you could try asking yourself if your emotion fits into one of these four (almost rhyming) categories: mad, sad, glad, and afraid. These are terms I use with clients as a helpful starting point for distinguishing basic emotions, but gradually you can work on getting more specific; emotions lists can also be helpful.

Chapter 28:
6 Ways To Achieve Peak Performance

To be successful requires much more than just your intelligence and talent. There are basic needs which have to be met to function at your peak. These basic needs are neglected by most, impairing their capacity to rise to those elusive higher levels of success and happiness in life.

1. Get enough sleep

Sleep deprivation means peak performance deprivation. Without proper sleep you wake up to meet the day feeling scatterbrained, foggy and unfocused. You grab your cup of coffee to get a charge on your brain, which completely depletes your brain function over the course of the day, making your brain even more exhausted.

Good sleep improves your ability to be patient, retain information, think clearly, make good decisions and be present and alert in all your daily interactions. Sleep is your time off from problem solving.

When you get the proper rest your brain becomes awake, alive and ready to generate the cognitive prowess and emotional regulation you need to function at your peak performance.

2. Drink lemon water

Lemon water is a great substitute for your morning coffee. Although lemons do not contain caffeine, lemon water has excellent pick-me-up properties without negative side effects. It energizes the brain, especially if it is warm, and hydrates your lymph system.

Among the most important benefits of lemon water are its strong antibacterial, antiviral, and immune-boosting power, making sick days from work nearly non-existent. Lemon water cures headache, freshens breath, cleanses the skin, improves digestion, eliminates PMS with its diuretic properties and reduces the acidity in the body.

Most importantly, lemon water increases your cognitive capacity and improves mood with its stimulating properties on the brain, helping you to operate more consistently in your peak performance zone.

3. Get daily exercise

Exercise is the best way to reduce the stress that impairs your performance stamina. Exercise increases your "happy" mood chemicals through the release of endorphins. Endorphins help rid your mind and body of tension alleviating anxiety helping you to calm down.

The brain needs physical activity to stay flexible. Exercise stimulates neurogenesis, or the growth of new brain cells, which improves overall brain function. The development of new brain cells keeps your brain young and in shape, allowing you to be more efficient, pliable and clear in your decision making, higher thinking and learning capacities. Neurogenesis is the catalyst to peak performance.

Further, there is nothing that can bring down self-esteem quicker than not liking how you look. Exercise improves self-confidence and your perception of your attractiveness and self-worth. This confidence contributes greatly to your success, prompting people to respect you and take you seriously

4. Have emotional support

Having healthy, loving relationships increases your happiness, success and longevity by promoting your capacity to function in life as your best self. Social connectedness and love gives you relationships to be motivated for and people to be inspired by.

A strong social network decreases stress, provides you with a sense of belonging and gives your life the deeper meaning it needs. When you are loved and loving, and carving out quality time to cultivate these relationships, you are exalted, elevated and encouraged to live your dreams fully.

5. Be unapologetically optimistic

A requirement of peak performance is to look for the best in every situation. Optimism is the commitment to believe, expect and trust that things in life are rigged in your favor. Even when something bad happens, you find the silver lining.

A positive outlook on life strengthens your immune system and the emotional quality of your life experiences, allowing you to be resilient in the face of fear, stress and challenge.

Being an optimist or a pessimist boils down to the way you talk to yourself. When you are optimistic you are fierce in the belief it is your own actions which result in positive things happening. You live by positive affirmation, take responsibility for your own happiness and anticipate more good things will happen for you in the future.

When bad things happen you do not blame yourself, you are simply willing to change yourself.

6. Have time alone

Time alone is refueling to your physical, mental, emotional and spiritual self. This time recharges you, helping to cultivate your peak performance levels again and again. You must give yourself time to recover from the stress of consistently being around others. Being around people continuously wears down your ability to regulate your emotional state, causing self-regulation fatigue. For this reason you must give yourself permission to take the pressure off and disconnect.

Chapter 29:
10 Stress Management Tips

Most students experience significant amounts of stress, and this stress can take a significant toll on health, happiness, and grades. For example, a study found that teens report stress levels similar to that of adults. Stress can affect health-related behaviors like sleep patterns, diet, and exercise as well, taking a larger toll. Given that nearly half of the survey respondents reported completing three hours of homework per night in addition to their full day of school work and extracurriculars, this is understandable.

1. Get Enough Sleep

Students, with their packed schedules, are notorious for missing sleep. Unfortunately, operating in a sleep-deprived state puts you at a distinct disadvantage. You're less productive, you may find it more difficult to learn, and you may even be a hazard behind the wheel. Don't neglect your sleep schedule. Aim to get at least 8 hours a night and take power naps when you need them.

2. Practice Visualization

Using guided imagery to reduce stress is easy and effective. Visualizations can help you calm down, detach from what's stressing you, and turn off your body's stress response. You can also use visualizations to prepare for presentations and score higher on tests by vividly seeing yourself performing just as you'd like to.

3. Exercise Regularly

One of the healthiest ways to blow off steam is to get regular exercise. Students can work exercise into their schedules by doing yoga in the morning, walking or biking to campus, or reviewing for tests with a friend while walking on a treadmill at the gym. Starting now and keeping a regular exercise practice throughout your lifetime can help you live longer and enjoy your life more.

4. Take Calming Breaths

When your body is experiencing a stress response, you're often not thinking as clearly as you could be. A quick way to calm down is to practice breathing exercises. These can be done virtually anywhere to relieve stress in minutes, and are especially effective for reducing anxiety before or even during tests, as well as during other times when stress feels overwhelming.

5. Practice Progressive Muscle Relaxation (PMR)

Another great stress reliever that can be used during tests, before bed, or at other times when stress has you physically wound up is progressive muscle relaxation (PMR). This technique involves tensing and relaxing all muscles until the body is completely relaxed.

With practice, you can learn to release stress from your body in seconds. This can be particularly helpful for students because it can be adapted to help relaxation efforts before sleep for deeper sleep, something students can always use, or even to relax and reverse test-induced panic before or during a test.

6. Listen to Music

A convenient stress reliever that has also shown many cognitive benefits, music can help you to relieve stress and either calm yourself down or stimulate your mind as your situation warrants. Students can harness the [benefits of music](#) by playing classical music while studying, playing upbeat music to "wake up" mentally, or relaxing with the help of their favorite slow melodies.

7. Get Organized

Clutter can cause stress, decrease productivity, and even cost you money. Many students live in a cluttered place, and this can have negative effects on grades. One way to reduce the amount of stress that you experience is to keep a minimalist, soothing study area that's free of distractions and clutter.

This can help lower stress levels, save time in finding lost items, and keep roommate relationships more positive. It can also help students gain a positive feeling about their study area, which helps with test prep and encourages more studying. It's worth the effort.

8. Eat a Healthy Diet

You may not realize it, but your diet can either boost your brainpower or sap you of mental energy. A healthy diet can function as both a stress management technique and a study aid. Improving your diet can keep you from experiencing diet-related mood swings, light-headedness, and more.

9. Try Self-Hypnosis

Students often find themselves "getting very sleepy" (like when they pull all-nighters), but—all kidding aside—self-hypnosis can be an effective stress management tool and a powerful productivity tool as well.

With it, you can help yourself release tension from your body and stress from your mind, and plant the seeds of success in your subconscious mind with the power of autosuggestion.

10. Use Positive Thinking and Affirmations

Did you know that [optimists](#) actually experience better circumstances, in part, because their way of thinking helps to *create* better circumstances in their lives? It's true! The habit of optimism and [positive thinking](#) can bring better health, baetter relationships, and, yes, better grades.

Learn how to train your brain for more positive self-talk and a brighter future with [affirmations](#) and other tools for optimism. You can also learn the limitations to affirmations and the caveats of positive thinking so you aren't working against yourself.

Chapter 30:
How To Deal With Impatience

"The big challenge with impatience is that it's largely justifiable. The way you respond, however, may not be." - Matt Christensen.

Why is he talking so loudly? Why is she walking so slowly? Why isn't he doing his chores? We have all been hit with the impatient nerve now and then. Although these situations aren't avoidable, how we deal and communicate with them counts in the end. The impatience that vibrates through our body can easily make us angry or result in other unpleasant reactions. It can get triggered by a phrase, behavior, or task that often stems from strength, anxiety, or related outside factors. Becoming more patient takes more time.

Dealing with impatience is surely hectic, but it's not that difficult once you master some techniques. The first thing to do when you're being impatient is to take several deep breaths. Our brains tend to go into a fight or flight situation whenever they sniff danger. As a result, hyperventilation or shortage of oxygen occurs. You start getting more excited and stressed and take quick, short breaths that do more harm than good. The best solution is to give yourself time and take a few seconds to breathe deeply. Catch your impatience with a productive response by calming and controlling your mind and body.

The next thing after relaxing your mind is to relax your muscles. When you feel impatient, give attention to your muscles by doing progressive muscle relaxation. Sit comfortably in a position and meditate. Stretch your arms and legs, and then stretch all of your tensed points one by one. Try to relax as much as you can. You will end up feeling calm, and the feeling of impatience will vanish.

We have all heard how communication is the key to dealing with almost everything. It can be fulfilling and productive to speak up about what's making you impatient and what's bothering you. But beware! It would help if you practiced tact and finesse to make sure you don't sound like a jerk when talking about your impatience-ness. Voicing your views out loud is an essential step in combating impatience. Acknowledging your feelings would also open doors for you to ask for help.

Impatience also thrives on disconnection. If not given the appropriate validation, it can be a recipe for a meltdown. Validation, both verbal and non-verbal responses, can communicate understanding, which can further facilitate connection. Validation can taper your impatience by helping shape your behavior and communication.

Dwelling on the feeling of being impatient can get you nowhere. It doesn't provide you with any sense of productiveness, helpfulness, or pleasantness. Rather than being caught up in the immediate goal, we must keep reminding ourselves to keep a larger perspective of the situation.

Always be mindful of your situations and trust your instinct to deal with your problems. Some people become impatient because of underlying unresolved issues, such as anger, perfectionism, and depression/anxiety. Try helping yourself with acceptance and commitment therapy, anger management, or CBT if you think you are caught up in these feelings. Remember, being patient can get you so many places, while being impatient will have you stuck in one!

Chapter 31:
How To Tell It's Time To Move On From Your Job Or Switch Careers

Making the decision to move on from your job is never easy. However, if you're a skilled professional who's looking for a new role, there's a vast range of opportunities available, and the team at Huxley are here to help you. We took a look at some of the key signs that could suggest it's time for you to seriously start considering your options.

You work to live, you don't live to work. While most jobs will involve the occasional late night in the office, if you're constantly starting work at seven in the morning, and not leaving until eight at night, it could be time to re-evaluate. At Huxley, we have numerous jobs available that offer a variety of flexible working options, and can find a job that has the right package for you.

You work hard so you can enjoy a lifestyle you deserve. And if you don't feel you're being paid fairly, it's time to look elsewhere and find a company that will value your worth. We can give you access to a range of positions with competitive salaries across IT, Engineering, Energy, and Banking and Finance.

The biggest reason people leave their job is due to a lack of opportunities for progression. Staying in a job for too long with no development isn't only de-motivating, it can also leave hiring managers questioning your credibility. Perhaps you're seeing others getting promoted around you? Or, more worryingly, is there a distinct lack of progression within your team? If alarm bells are ringing, it's probably time to check out, and move somewhere you'll really be appreciated.

Some people go to work, do their job, and go home. And that's fine. But do you ever find yourself wishing you were more involved in a team? Or shared similar values to your organisation? If so, maybe the culture of your company isn't right for you. At Huxley, our consultants work hard to learn as much as possible about you. This allows us to not just to match you with the right job, but to find a company and team that are right for you.

For ambitious professionals, personal growth and development is extremely important. If you feel like you've learned everything you can within your role, then it's probably time to move on. Your job should challenge, motivate, and offer you the opportunity to continuously learn new skills. At Huxley, we have a range of roles available with companies of all sizes that offer a variety of development programmes to ensure you're constantly learning, and getting something extra out of your job.

When all is said and done, if the time has come to move on – you'll know. Just as there's no perfect timing, there's no right or wrong reason for quitting your job. You know yourself better than anyone else. And if you're ready to go, we're here for you.

Whatever your reasons for wanting to make a move, Huxley are here to help. Our dedicated consultants are on hand to offer personalised advice, and work in partnership with all candidates we place. By gaining a comprehensive understanding of your needs and desires, we can find a job that offers the career satisfaction you deserve.

Chapter 32:
How To Play The Long Game In Life

Playing the long game in life is forming or shaping your life so that you control certain aspects of it. You should constantly strive for self-improvement and try to push yourself a little more each day. You are starting your day early and making sure that this day fulfills most of our tasks. Build strategies for career growth and development. Also, make sPlaying the long game in life is taking control of your future in a way that everything is planned. You have to be mindful of everything. Identifying what makes you happy, energized, and focused is a chance to prepare everything for the long term. To form the long game in your life means taking small steps of success in life for yourself. You need to strategize every move of yours.

It would be best if you were above average in gaining knowledge to predict the outcome of your move. If you want to plan long-term success in life, you need to understand the situations according to your needs. Always keep your mind open for excessive knowledge. Be hungry for it. Take steps towards self-improvement. Socialize with people who are more knowledgeable or experienced than you are. Learning should always be one of the priorities. Challenge yourself for more daily. As it's said, "if you are the smartest person in the room, you are in the wrong room." Understand that you will always need more to expand in life and be successful in life.

It would be best to keep in mind that not every step of yours will go as planned. Get yourself ready for rejection. You should not be scared of getting a rejection, but take it as a constructive opportunity to build yourself stronger for the next time. Your part should be fulfilled correctly. Hard work should be done, and the right choices should be made. In this case, advice should be taken too. You should not completely rely on someone, but a companion can be comforting. Always appreciate your co-workers and superior. That will help you in the future and your long-term game for success in life. Just keep in mind that the fear of rejection is useless.

Shaping your path is a difficult task and a very important opportunity. When you are forming your way of life, one of the most important things will be the type of people you will meet. You should be careful about the kind of people that surround you. As it is said, "one bad company can ruin all." This is true in a sense. Keep supportive and smart people by your side. Your long-term friendship or relationship can affect your life in many ways. It may change the outcome completely. Now, we would not want just anyone to come and take that part. That is why choosing the best people to surround you matters the most.
ure to have lots of fun in between the work. In the end, your hard work will pay off, and everything will feel like it was worth doing all the work for.

Chapter 33:
16 Steps To Stop Feeling Like Shit

We all have days where we feel like absolute crap and don't even feel like talking to anyone. There are some small steps that can help you feel better even if its just for a while.

1. Get a drink of water

You could be dehydrated! Your body needs water. Not juice, soda, or alcohol — get a tall glass of water and make yourself drink all of it.

2. Make your bed

When you have a lot to do and it feels overwhelming, making your bed can be the first step in getting your life on track. It will also (hopefully) discourage you from getting back into it.

3. Take a shower

Life feels different when you're clean! And it can give you a burst of energy if you're feeling lethargic. Wash your hair and give yourself a head massage.

4. Have a snack — not junk food!

Did you eat enough today? It's super tempting to eat junk food when you feel like crap. If you don't feel like making a whole meal, maybe eat just a piece of fruit; something you can burn throughout the day and not in a burst of five minutes.

5. Take a walk.

You might need some fresh air and not even know it. Give your body some natural light, breathe some different air, move your legs a little, even if it's for just five minutes. Allow yourself to think some different thoughts.

6. Change your clothes

Even if you aren't going to leave the house today, put on real clothes. Or, if you've been wearing the same uncomfortable clothes all day and feel restless, change into your sleepy clothes and slippers and relax.

7. Change your environment

Staring at the same four walls day after day can be drudging. Can you work from a cafe, a library, or a friend's house? If you can add going somewhere to the list of things you did today, you may feel more accomplished.

8. Talk to someone, not on the internet — it can be about anything

If you don't feel like talking through your troubles, that's OK. Visit a friend, talk to them about a movie you saw. Call your mom and see how she's doing.

9. Dance to an upbeat guilty pleasure song

NOT ELLIOT SMITH! Pick something high energy and bump it. Dance like a rock star for one song to get your blood pumping again.

10. Get some exercise

Do some cardio, work up a sweat. If you don't have the time for a whole workout, look up a sun salutation on YouTube and stretch for as long as you have time. Do some push-ups or sit-ups at your desk.

11. Accomplish something — even if it's something tiny

Do you need to grab some groceries? Schedule a doctor's appointment? Reply to an email? If you can't get to the big stuff on your list, focus on the small stuff, and don't forget to congratulate yourself for getting something done.

12. Hug an animal.

If you don't have a pet, can you visit a friend's? Or can you go to an animal shelter?

13. Make a "done" list instead of a "to-do" list.

Instead of overwhelming yourself right now, start feeling better about what you did get done. You can add "brushed teeth," "washed dishes," or "picked out an outfit" to your list. It doesn't matter how small the task, prove to yourself that you're effectual.

14. Watch a YouTube video that always makes you laugh

I personally recommend this one.

15. Give yourself permission to feel shitty

You're allowed to have a shitty day, and you don't have to fix it all right now. If you try to fix it and it doesn't work, that doesn't mean it's hopeless. Give yourself the time and space you need to feel what you're feeling.

16. Shut yourself off from social media or socialization for a short while

Do you get comparison syndrome, or just me? You too? Cool.

So I need to shut up social media sometimes so I'm not comparing the highlights of someone else's life, to my own life. People seem like they have it all, and they don't spend their evenings sitting in the dark, eating a whole pizza by themselves… which is not true. Other people have their own demons. You just rarely see it on social media.

I turned myself off from social media for a while, in order to help myself. I stop comparing my life to the lives of others who seem to have it all.

Chapter 34:
20 Affirmations For Women

If you are like me you know there is only so much you can control throughout the day. What I can control is the way you think and how I perceive the world around you. Sometimes it's easy to let the stress of the world seep in and affect your mindset.

That said, with the help of positive affirmations you can improve not only your mood but your outlook on life. So in this article, I'll quickly explain the power of affirmations and give you 20 positive affirmations for women.

1. I feel the love of others who are not around me.

2. I am an amazing gift to myself, my friends, and the world. I am too much of an amazing gift to feel self-pity.

3. I love and appreciate myself. I am who I am and I love myself.

4. I do not need the company of others to feel complete. I am more than enough. I enjoy being in my own solitude.

5. The past no longer matters. It has no control over me. What only matters is the present. What I do in the present will shape my future. The past has no say in this.

6. Everything that I need will be provided to me at the right time and the right place. When something is meant to happen it will happen.

7. It is too early to give up on my dreams. it is always too early to give up on my dreams.

8. I will not give up until I have tried everything. And when I have tried everything I will look for other ways to try.

9. I believe in myself and I believe in the path I have chosen. I cannot choose the obsticles in my way, but I can choose to continue on my path, because it leads to my goals.

10. I am not only enough, I am more than enough. I also get better every day I live. Tomorrow I will be a better version of myself than I was today.

11. I will not criticize myself. I will love myself for who I am and for what I have become.

12. I will award and praise myself for my accomplishments. I will not dwell on the praise of others for my own praise is more than enough.

13. I will not compare myself to anyone else because everyone is on their own personal journeys. My journey is unique and cannot be compared.

14. I will only compare myself to myself. I know what greatness I can accomplish and I will only hold myself to that.

15. I will not look at the darkness in the world around me but instead at the light that is within me.

16. I am happy with who I am. I am happy I am in my own skin. I am enough and I do not need to be someone else.

17. The answer is always in front of me, even if I have not yet seen it. As long as I continued to search I will find the answer.

18. Every problem I ever face will have a solution. There has never been a question without an answer. I just need to discover the answer.

19. I am a smart, capable, brilliant woman, and I have everything I need to get through this. When I make it through this I will be better for it.

20. Those who love me will always love me, even if they do not fully understand my dreams. True friends and family will love me regardless of what my dreams. False friends will love me because of my dreams.

You don't need to repeat every single one of these positive affirmations throughout the course of a day. Chances are you don't have the time, and you may not need some of them (at least not currently. Instead, you need to:

- Take a few moments out of your day to breathe while repeating some of your favorite affirmations.
- Say the affirmations out loud. It works better if you hear them spoken.
- If you keep a journal you can write meaningful affirmations down. Much like saying the affirmations out loud, writing them down helps make it feel more real (than simply thinking them).
- Use the affirmations often. There's no such thing as too many affirmations.

I hope you've found some of these affirmations helpful. Give them a try. I know many have helped me over the years. And if you want to learn more about how to boost your physical and mental wellbeing make sure to check out another one of my affirmation blogs right here!

www.ingramcontent.com/pod-product-compliance
Lightning Source LLC
Chambersburg PA
CBHW072204100526
44589CB00015B/2366